THE
LIBRARY OF BATS™

PLAIN-NOSED BATS

EMILY RAABE

The Rosen Publishing Group's
PowerKids Press™
New York

For my mother and her attic full of little brown bats

Published in 2003 by The Rosen Publishing Group, Inc.
29 East 21st Street, New York, NY 10010

PLEASE NOTE: Although most bats are harmless, if you see a bat lying on the ground, do not pick it up or touch it. Bats are wild animals and they could carry rabies or other diseases.

First Edition

Editor: Natashya Wilson
Book Design: Emily Muschinske

Photo Credits: Cover, title page, pp. 13, 15 © Michael Durham; pp. 4, 8, 19 © Roger Rageot/David Liebman; pp. 5 (top), 16, 21 (lower left and right) © Roger W. Barbour/National Museum of Natural History/Smithsonian Institution; p. 7 © Albert Visage/Peter Arnold, Inc.; pp. 5 (bottom), 6 (inset) 12, 15 (inset) © Merlin D. Tuttle, Bat Conservation International; pp. 6, 9 (left and center), 10, 11, 17, 18, 21 (center), 22 © Robert & Linda Mitchell; p. 9 (map) Eric DePalo.

Raabe, Emily.
Plain-nosed bats / by Emily Raabe.
    p. cm. — (The library of bats)
Includes bibliographical references (p.   ).
Summary: Describes the appearance, habitat, and behavior of members of the plain-nosed bat family.
ISBN 0-8239-6323-3 (lib. bdg.)
1. Vespertilionidae—Juvenile literature. [1. Plain-nosed bats. 2. Bats.] I. Title.
QL737.C595 R33 2003
2001006032—dc21   2001006032

Manufactured in the United States of America

CONTENTS

Bats Around the World

You can find bats almost anywhere in the world. In fact the only **continent** on which you won't find bats is Antarctica! Bats live in deserts, in forests, and in the mountains. Some bats live on islands. There are nearly 1,000 **species**, or kinds, of bats in the world. Scientists group these species of bats into **families** to study them. There are 17 families of bats. Some families are small. The smoky bat family has only two species in it. The largest family of bats is the plain-nosed bat family. There are about 300 species in this family. Plain-nosed bats are the most common bats in Europe and in North America.

These two bats are plain-nosed bats. The bat on the bottom is a little brown bat. The bat on the top is an Allen's big-eared bat.

Bat Fact

Bats have been around for at least 50 million years. Today there are 17 families of bats. Fifty million years ago, there were only 11 families. Six of these original families of bats still exist. These families are the sheath-tailed bats, the false vampire bats, the horseshoe bats, the leaf-nosed bats, the nataloid bats, and the plain-nosed bats.

4

WHAT IS A PLAIN-NOSED BAT?

How would you recognize a plain-nosed bat? If you see a small, brown bat with big ears and a small nose, then you are probably looking at a plain-nosed bat. Plain-nosed bats are usually brown or gray, although some of them are silver, orange, red, or yellow. The spotted bat, a kind of plain-nosed bat, is black with white spots. Plain-nosed bats have small eyes, but their ears are usually quite large. Some plain-nosed bats' ears can be nearly 2 inches (5 cm) long. That's pretty big when you consider that plain-nosed bats' bodies are only from 1 to 3 inches (2.5–8 cm) long!

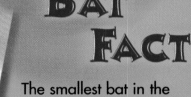

BAT FACT

The smallest bat in the world is the bumblebee bat of Thailand. The bumblebee bat weighs ½₀ of an ounce (1.5 g) and is smaller than your thumb! The largest bat in the world is the flying fox *(above)* of Southeast Asia. This bat weighs up to 3 pounds (1.5 kg). Its wingspan can reach 5 ½ feet (1.5 m)!

This long-eared brown bat has small lumps above its nose, but don't be fooled. It is a plain-nosed bat. Compare its nose with the fancy leaf-shaped nose of the Australian false vampire bat (inset).

7

WHERE DO PLAIN-NOSED BATS LIVE?

There may be plain-nosed bats living in your backyard or even in the attic of your house. Most plain-nosed bats live in caves. They also live in mines, wells, tunnels, trees, and buildings. Many female plain-nosed bats choose to raise their babies in the warm attics of houses.

Plain-nosed bats eat insects as food. In the winter, insects are hard to find. Some plain-nosed bats fly south for the winter. This is called **migration**. However, most plain-nosed bats deal with winter by sleeping right

BAT STATS

Plain-nosed bats hibernate in larger groups than they live in when they are awake. A cave was found in Vermont that had 300,000 hibernating little brown bats!

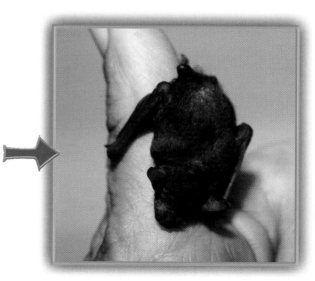

Little brown bats are smaller than an adult person's thumb.

through it! This long sleep is called **hibernation**. Most plain-nosed bats have special winter caves where they go to hibernate every year.

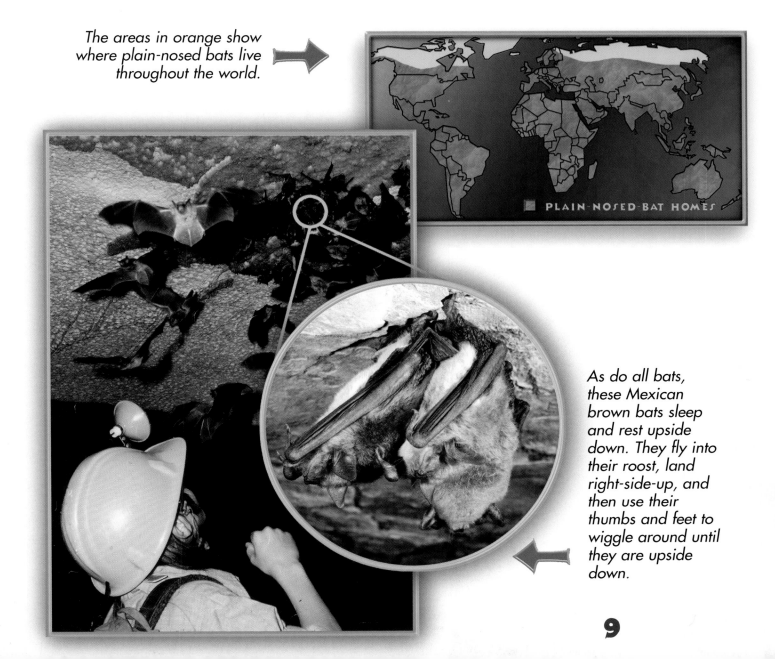

The areas in orange show where plain-nosed bats live throughout the world.

PLAIN-NOSED-BAT HOMES

As do all bats, these Mexican brown bats sleep and rest upside down. They fly into their roost, land right-side-up, and then use their thumbs and feet to wiggle around until they are upside down.

9

Bat Fact

It is dangerous for hibernating bats to be woken up. If a hibernating bat is frightened into flying, it can use up to 30 days worth of the fat that it needs to hibernate. This means that the bat might starve to death before the winter is over. Today many hibernation caves are protected from people.

10

When a plain-nosed bat is ready to hibernate, it first has to find the right place. The right place for most bats is in a cave. The cave needs to be cold, but not freezing. Plain-nosed bats sometimes fly hundreds of miles (km) to find just the right cave. When a bat finds the cave, it will snuggle in and hang upside down with other plain-nosed bats. Then the bat will slowly let its body **temperature** drop until it is the same as the temperature in the cave. The bat also slows down its heart rate and its breathing. During hibernation bats live on fat stored in their bodies. Bats can hibernate all winter long.

This hibernating hummingbird bat is covered in dew. The dew helps to keep the bat's body from running out of water, or dehydrating.

INSECT CATCHERS

Almost all plain-nosed bats eat insects. They have a very good system for catching insects. Using its wings, a plain-nosed bat will knock a flying insect into a pocket that is formed by the bat's tail and the skin that covers the tail. The bat then tucks its nose and mouth into its tail pocket to get the insect, often turning a full somersault in the air! Once the bat has the insect in its mouth, it will hang upside down somewhere and munch up its meal. Then it will take to the sky again, hunting for more bugs. Plain-nosed bats help to keep down insect **populations**. A little brown bat can eat more than 500 mosquito-size insects in an hour!

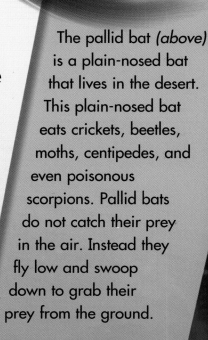

BAT FACT

The pallid bat (above) is a plain-nosed bat that lives in the desert. This plain-nosed bat eats crickets, beetles, moths, centipedes, and even poisonous scorpions. Pallid bats do not catch their prey in the air. Instead they fly low and swoop down to grab their prey from the ground.

The skin around this little brown bat's tail forms the pouch in which the bat catches its insect meals.

13

Hunting by Sound

Plain-nosed bats are not blind. However, as do most bats, they hunt at night. They find their insect meals in the dark by using something called **echolocation**. During echolocation, bats make sounds through either their mouths or their noses. The sounds bounce off any objects that are in the way. A bat listens to how long it takes a sound to return. This tells the bat how far away an object is. Some echolocation cries are loud. Some are quiet. One type of bat in the leaf-nosed bat family whispers its cries so that it can sneak up on insects without being heard. Little brown bats scream their cries. Like a dog whistle, the cries of little brown bats are too high for humans to hear. If we could hear the cries, they would sound as loud as a fire alarm!

Bat Stats

As bats get closer to the insects they hunt, they cry out more often. A hoary bat may go from making 3–10 cries per second to making 200 cries per second.

A western long-eared bat drinks from a pond. Inset: *These lines represent a little brown bat's cry. The sound bounces off an insect, telling the bat where the insect is.*

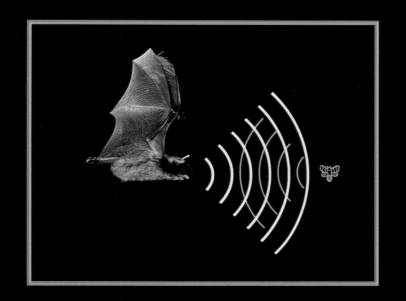

BIG-EARED BATS

Plain-nosed bats might have plain noses, but there is nothing plain about their ears! Some plain-nosed bats have truly huge ears. Most of the big-eared bats hunt insects on the ground instead of in the air. As they get close to the ground, these big-eared bats stop echolocating. Instead they listen for insects to rustle in the grass. To hear insects move, these bats have to have wonderful ears. Allen's big-eared bats live in the Southwest of the United States. These plain-nosed bats' ears can be 1½ inches (4 cm) long. Some big-eared bats' ears are so big that they fold them down at night!

BAT FACT

Unlike most big-eared bats, spotted bats (above) do not grab insects from the ground. Instead spotted bats eat mostly moths that they catch in the air. Scientists think that spotted bats have huge ears so that they can echolocate over long distances. A spotted bat's cry can bounce off objects that are 800 feet (244 m) away.

16

Long-eared bats move their ears forward to listen for insects. They can fold them down to tuck them out of the way (inset) when they rest.

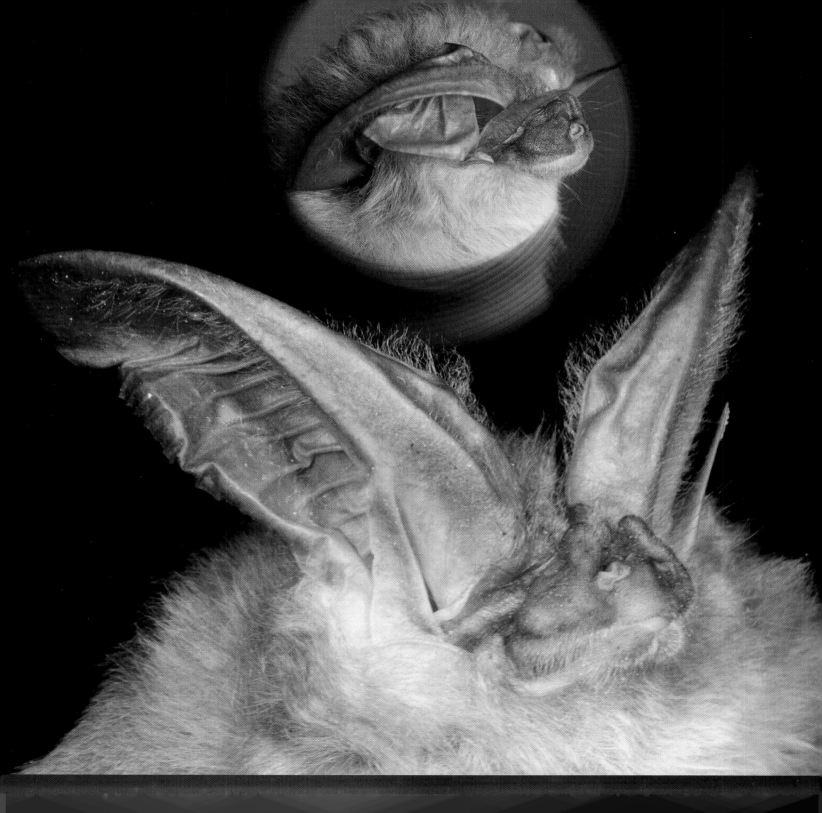

THE BAT IN YOUR BACKYARD

If you have ever seen a bat in your backyard, chances are that it was a little brown bat. This plain-nosed bat lives throughout North America. Little brown bats weigh from ¼ to ½ ounce (7–14 g) and are covered in soft, brown fur. The long hair on their feet covers their toes. Little brown bats use echolocation to catch insects in the air. In one summer, a **colony** of 100 little brown bats can eat 42 pounds (19 kg) of insects. This is good news for humans. The not-so-good news is that little brown bats like to live in houses. Some people don't like sharing their attics with bats. Other people like having bats around to eat pesky insects!

 There are 97 different species of little brown bats. This colony of Mexican brown bats lives in Panther Cave.

BAT FACT

Little brown bats spend their summers in caves, old mines, or buildings. These summer colonies are made up of either male little brown bats or females and their babies. In the winter, little brown bats hibernate in cold caves, far under the ground. The winter colonies are made up of both male and female bats, all hibernating together.

19

Colorful Plain-Nosed Bats

Although most plain-nosed bats are brown, a few types have bright coloring. The eastern red bat is covered in reddish orange fur. This bat lives in eastern Canada and the eastern United States. The woolly bat, also called the painted bat, is a plain-nosed bat that is found in Africa, India, and Australia. This bat can be bright red or orange. Woolly bats' wings are black with orange stripes. These bats are covered with long, woolly hair, like curly-haired sheep. Silver-haired bats have soft, black fur with silver tips. These beautiful bats are common in North America during the summer. In the fall and the spring, they can be found in the southern part of the United States. No one knows where silver-haired bats go in the winter!

Bat Stats

Hoary bat females can have up to 4 babies at a time. Red bat females have been found with 5 babies! The usual number of babies for both types of bats is from 2 to 3.

A hoary bat's (top) yellow fur is tipped with gray. This can help a hoary bat (bottom left) blend in with trees. Red bat (right) males are often brighter than red bat females.

20

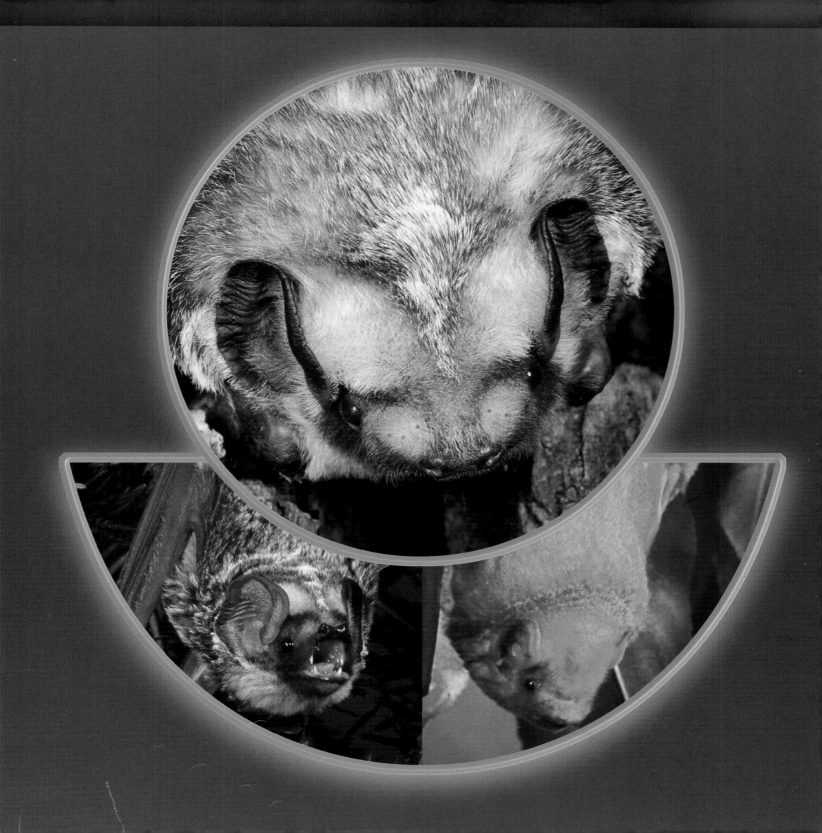

Plain-Nosed Bats in Danger

Plain-nosed bats can live for 30 years, but they face many dangers. In the past, thousands of bats were killed in their caves by people who saw them as pests. Today people are beginning to realize how important bats are for keeping insect populations under control. However, even people who like bats do not always like sharing their houses with them. One way to keep bats out of people's houses is to build bat houses. A bat house looks like a large birdhouse. It is often placed on the roof of a barn or on top of a tall pole. You can buy a bat house at a pet store, or you can build one yourself. Building a bat house is a great way to invite bats to live near you and to eat your bugs!

Bat Fact

Plain-nosed bats often eat insects that have been sprayed with poisonous chemicals. These chemicals, called pesticides, build up in bats' bodies and kill them. When bats and other animals die from eating chemicals, it is a warning to humans that we need to clean up our planet.

22

Glossary

colony (KAH-luh-nee) A group of people or animals living in the same place.

continent (KON-tin-ent) A large body of land. Scientists divide Earth into seven continents.

echolocation (eh-koh-loh-KAY-shun) A method of locating objects by producing a sound and judging the time it takes the echo to return and the direction from which it returns. Bats, dolphins, porpoises, killer whales, and some shrews all use echolocation.

families (FAM-leez) The scientific names for large groups of plants or animals that are alike in some ways.

hibernation (hy-bur-NAY-shun) To spend the winter in a sleeplike state, with heart rate and breathing slowed down.

migration (my-GRAY-shun) When groups of animals travel to find food or to escape cold weather.

populations (pah-pyoo-LAY-shunz) The numbers of each kind of creature living in a place.

species (SPEE-sheez) A single kind of plant or animal. Humans are one species.

temperature (TEM-pruh-cher) The heat in a living body.

INDEX

WEB SITES

To learn more about plain-nosed bats, other bats, or building a bat house, check out these Web sites:

www.batcon.org
www.discovery.com/news/features/bats/bats.html